BIBLE Says about

WORSHIP

What the BIBLE Says about WORSHIP

© 2009 by Barbour Publishing, Inc.

ISBN 978-1-60260-280-9

All rights reserved. No part of this publication may be reproduced or transmitted for commercial purposes, except for brief quotations in printed reviews, without written permission of the publisher.

Scripture quotations marked NIV are taken from the HOLY BIBLE, NEW INTERNATIONAL VERSION®. NIV®. Copyright © 1973, 1978, 1984 by International Bible Society. Used by permission of Zondervan. All rights reserved.

Scripture quotations marked NASB are taken from the New American Standard Bible, © 1960, 1962, 1963, 1968, 1971, 1972, 1973, 1975, 1977, 1995 by The Lockman Foundation. Used by permission.

Scripture quotations marked NLT are taken from the *Holy Bible*, New Living Translation, copyright © 1996, 2004. Used by permission of Tyndale House Publishers, Inc. Wheaton, Illinois 60189, U.S.A. All rights reserved.

Scripture quotations marked CEV are taken from the Contemporary English Version, Copyright © 1991, 1992, 1995 by the American Bible Society. Used by permission.

Scripture quotations marked NKJV are from the New King James Version®. Copyright © 1982 by Thomas Nelson, Inc. Used by permission. All rights reserved.

Scripture quotations marked MSG are taken from *THE MESSAGE*. Copyright © by Eugene H. Peterson 1993, 1994, 1995, 1996, 2000, 2001, 2002. Used by permission of NavPress Publishing Group.

Scripture quotations marked ESV are from The Holy Bible, English Standard Version®, copyright © 2001 by Crossway Bibles, a publishing ministry of Good News Publishers. Used by permission. All rights reserved.

Scripture quotations marked KJV are taken from the King James Version of the Bible.

Published by Barbour Publishing, Inc., P.O. Box 719, Uhrichsville, Ohio 44683, www.barbourbooks.com

Our mission is to publish and distribute inspirational products offering exceptional value and biblical encouragement to the masses.

Printed in the United States of America

CONTENTS

Introduction: Getting Everything Straight......9

1. Why We Worship......................11
   Worship Him because He Is Worthy....12
   Worship Is Commanded..............16
   Worship Blesses Us..................20
   Worship Encourages Others..........25

2. The Focus of Our Worship............31
   Worship the One and Only God.......32
   Worship the Great One..............39
   Worship the Holy One...............43
   Worship the Creator of Everything...45
   Worship the Ruler of All.............51
   Worship the Living God..............55
   Worship the Approachable Father....57

3. Who Should Worship God.............63
   Worship Is Due from Everyone.......64
   Worship Is Offered by Creation......68
   Worship Is Given by Angels..........72
   Worship Is Encouraged from Children...75
   Worship Is Presented by His People...77

WHAT THE BIBLE SAYS ABOUT WORSHIP

4. How We Should Worship 83
Worship with Constant Praise 84
Worship with Great Joy 87
Worship with Reverent Fear 90
Worship with Grateful Hearts 93
Worship with the Spirit's Help 96

5. Worshipping God with Our Actions . . .101
Worship by Developing Your Gifts 102
Worship by Living Righteously 105
Worship by Giving 109
Worship by Caring for the Needy 110

6. Forms of Worship .115
Worship with Others 116
Worship with Song 119
Worship with Musical Instruments 122
Worship with What You Say 125
Worship with Reverent Posture 128
Worship with Dance 130
Worship with Prayer 132

WHAT THE BIBLE SAYS ABOUT WORSHIP

7. Personal Reasons to Worship God.....139
   - Worship Because of His Love..........140
   - Worship Because of His Answers to Prayer........................143
   - Worship Because of His Forgiveness...146
   - Worship Because of His Mercy and Grace......................150
   - Worship Because of His Salvation.....153
   - Worship Because of His Help.........157
   - Worship Because of His Comfort.....160
   - Worship Because of His Provision.....163
   - Worship Because of His Good Works.........................166
   - Worship Because of His Word........170
   - Worship Because of His Protection and Strength....................173

8. Examples of Worship................181
   - Worship Without Needing Social Approval......................182
   - Worship During Difficult Times........184

WHAT THE BIBLE SAYS ABOUT WORSHIP

Worship Through Grief 186
Worship on the Battlefield. 188
Worship Before a Great Undertaking . . 189

WHAT THE BIBLE SAYS ABOUT WORSHIP

INTRODUCTION
GETTING EVERYTHING STRAIGHT

In recent years, many have come to view worship as synonymous with "praise and worship" songs. This misconception leads some people to the conclusion that their worship each week exists solely within the realm of the songs they sing in church or certain music they listen to on their MP3 players.

God's Word, however, points us to an infinitely broader view of worship—one that encompasses everything we do. Our thoughts, prayers, words, actions, relationships, work—even our play—can become vehicles for worship if our hearts are tuned to worship God.

Read the pages that follow to have your view of worship challenged and expanded.

WHAT THE BIBLE SAYS ABOUT WORSHIP

CHAPTER 1
WHY WE WORSHIP

Right after a tragedy occurred in our community, I participated in what was probably the most impactful worship service of my life. In response to the tragedy, our church organized an impromptu service where we spent time praying and praising God. While I attended in an effort to support other community members who were directly affected by the tragedy, the service was surprisingly touching for me personally. As I worshipped God in prayer and song, He impressed upon me that He has the answers to the big "why" questions we all were asking. The reminder that God is still on the throne and that He knows what He's doing—even when I can't see it—proved to be a great comfort to me and gave me the hope I needed to be an encouragement to those around me.

■ Ellie, age 37, West Virginia ■

WHAT THE BIBLE SAYS ABOUT WORSHIP

WORSHIP HIM BECAUSE HE IS WORTHY

- The Lord is great and deserves
    our greatest praise!
  He is the only God
    worthy of our worship.

  1 Chronicles 16:25 CEV

- All the nations you have made shall come
  and worship before you, O Lord,
  and shall glorify your name.

  Psalm 86:9 ESV

- For great is the Lord and most worthy
  of praise; he is to be feared above
  all gods.

  Psalm 96:4 NIV

WHAT THE BIBLE SAYS ABOUT WORSHIP

- "You must fear the LORD your God and worship him and cling to him. Your oaths must be in his name alone. He alone is your God, the only one who is worthy of your praise, the one who has done these mighty miracles that you have seen with your own eyes."

  DEUTERONOMY 10:20–21 NLT

- We praise you, LORD God, and we worship you at your sacred mountain. Only you are God!

  PSALM 99:9 CEV

- Offer praise to God our Savior because of our Lord Jesus Christ! Only God can keep you from falling and make you pure and joyful in his glorious presence. Before time began and now and forevermore, God is worthy of glory, honor, power, and authority. Amen.

  JUDE 24–25 CEV

WHAT THE BIBLE SAYS ABOUT WORSHIP

- O nations of the world, recognize the Lord,
  recognize that the Lord is glorious
  and strong.
  Give to the Lord the glory he deserves!
  Bring your offering and come into his
  presence.
  Worship the Lord in all his holy splendor.

  1 Chronicles 16:28–29 NLT

- Praise be to the Lord God, the God of Israel,
  who alone does marvelous deeds.
  Praise be to his glorious name forever;
  may the whole earth be filled with
  his glory.
  Amen and Amen.

  Psalm 72:18–19 NIV

- "Dominion and awe belong to God;
  he establishes order in the heights
  of heaven."

  Job 25:2 NIV

WHAT THE BIBLE SAYS ABOUT WORSHIP

- In a loud voice they sang:
    "Worthy is the Lamb, who was slain,
    to receive power and wealth
    and wisdom and strength and honor
    and glory and praise!"

    REVELATION 5:12 NIV

WHAT THE BIBLE SAYS ABOUT WORSHIP

WORSHIP IS COMMANDED

- Then a voice came from the throne, saying:
  "Praise our God,
  all you his servants,
  you who fear him,
  both small and great!"

  REVELATION 19:5 NIV

- "Be still, and know that I am God;
  I will be exalted among the nations,
  I will be exalted in the earth."

  PSALM 46:10 NIV

- It is the LORD your God you must follow, and him you must revere. Keep his commands and obey him; serve him and hold fast to him.

  DEUTERONOMY 13:4 NIV

WHAT THE BIBLE SAYS ABOUT WORSHIP

- Give to the Lord the glory he deserves!
  Bring your offering and come into his courts.

  PSALM 96:8 NLT

- Praise be to the Lord, the God of Israel,
  from everlasting to everlasting.
  Let all the people say, "Amen!"
  Praise the Lord.

  PSALM 106:48 NIV

- Declare his glory among the nations,
  his marvelous deeds among all peoples.

  1 CHRONICLES 16:24 NIV

- Honor the Lord, you heavenly beings;
  honor the Lord for his glory and strength.

  PSALM 29:1 NLT

- Declare his glory among the nations,
  his marvelous works among all the peoples!

  PSALM 96:3 ESV

WHAT THE BIBLE SAYS ABOUT WORSHIP

- The Sovereign Lord will show his justice to
    the nations of the world.
  Everyone will praise him!
  His righteousness will be like a garden
    in early spring, with plants springing
    up everywhere.

  Isaiah 61:11 nlt

- So thank God for his marvelous love,
    for his miracle mercy to the children
    he loves.

  Psalm 107:31 msg

WHAT THE BIBLE SAYS ABOUT WORSHIP

■ But you are a chosen people, a royal priesthood, a holy nation, a people belonging to God, that you may declare the praises of him who called you out of darkness into his wonderful light.

1 Peter 2:9 NIV

WORSHIP BLESSES US

- Praise the LORD.
  Blessed is the man who fears the LORD,
  > who finds great delight in his commands.
  >> PSALM 112:1 NIV

- Blessed are all who fear the LORD,
  > who walk in his ways.
  You will eat the fruit of your labor;
  > blessings and prosperity will be yours.
  Your wife will be like a fruitful vine
  > within your house;
  > your sons will be like olive shoots
  > around your table.
  Thus is the man blessed
  > who fears the LORD.
  >> PSALM 128:1–4 NIV

WHAT THE BIBLE SAYS ABOUT WORSHIP

- What a stack of blessing you have piled up
  for those who worship you,
  Ready and waiting for all who run to you
  to escape an unkind world.

  PSALM 31:19 MSG

- Better is one day in your courts than a thousand elsewhere; I would rather be a doorkeeper in the house of my God than dwell in the tents of the wicked.

  PSALM 84:10 NIV

- Praise the LORD!
  How good to sing praises to our God!
  How delightful and how fitting!

  PSALM 147:1 NLT

WHAT THE BIBLE SAYS ABOUT WORSHIP

■ Blessed are those you choose
>and bring near to live in your courts!
>
>We are filled with the good things of your
>house, of your holy temple.

>PSALM 65:4 NIV

■ He will bless those who fear the LORD,
The small together with the great.

>PSALM 115:13 NASB

■ GOD's angel sets up a circle
>of protection around us while we pray....
>
>Worship GOD if you want the best;
>worship opens doors to all his goodness.

>PSALM 34:7, 9 MSG

WHAT THE BIBLE SAYS ABOUT WORSHIP

- "The Lord commanded us to obey all these decrees and to fear the Lord our God, so that we might always prosper and be kept alive, as is the case today."

    DEUTERONOMY 6:24 NIV

- You have made known to me the path of life; you will fill me with joy in your presence, with eternal pleasures at your right hand.

    PSALM 16:11 NIV

- Watch this: God's eye is on those who respect him, the ones who are looking for his love.

    PSALM 33:18 MSG

- No, the Lord's delight is in those who fear him, those who put their hope in his unfailing love.

    PSALM 147:11 NLT

WHAT THE BIBLE SAYS ABOUT WORSHIP

■ What a beautiful thing, GOD, to give thanks,
to sing an anthem to you, the High God!

PSALM 92:1 MSG

WHAT THE BIBLE SAYS ABOUT WORSHIP

WORSHIP ENCOURAGES OTHERS

■ When you meet together, sing psalms, hymns, and spiritual songs, as you praise the Lord with all your heart. Always use the name of our Lord Jesus Christ to thank God the Father for everything.

Ephesians 5:19–20 cev

■ Oh come, let us sing to the Lord;
    let us make a joyful noise to the
    rock of our salvation!
Let us come into his presence with
    thanksgiving; let us make a joyful noise
    to him with songs of praise!
For the Lord is a great God,
    and a great King above all gods.

Psalm 95:1–3 esv

WHAT THE BIBLE SAYS ABOUT WORSHIP

■ Listen! Your watchmen lift up their voices;
>together they shout for joy.
>
>When the Lord returns to Zion,
>they will see it with their own eyes.
>
>Burst into songs of joy together,
>you ruins of Jerusalem,
>for the Lord has comforted his people,
>he has redeemed Jerusalem.

Isaiah 52:8–9 niv

■ Let the message about Christ, in all its richness, fill your lives. Teach and counsel each other with all the wisdom he gives. Sing psalms and hymns and spiritual songs to God with thankful hearts.

Colossians 3:16 nlt

■ Glorify the Lord with me;
>let us exalt his name together.

Psalm 34:3 niv

WHAT THE BIBLE SAYS ABOUT WORSHIP

- We should keep on encouraging each other to be thoughtful and to do helpful things. Some people have gotten out of the habit of meeting for worship, but we must not do that. We should keep on encouraging each other, especially since you know that the day of the Lord's coming is getting closer.

    HEBREWS 10:24–25 CEV

ONE MOMENT AT A TIME

WORSHIPPING THE KING

- **Remember God's place.** When community and world events affect us in painful ways, it is helpful to remember that God is still king of the universe. He still sits on the throne and is in control—even when we don't understand what is happening.

- **Write a note.** Write a note to a missionary or friend encouraging them to remember and worship God in their work. As you think through how to encourage someone else, you'll find your own heart contemplating all the ways that God is worthy of your worship.

■ **Memorize a psalm.** Consider memorizing a psalm (or part of one) that can serve as a reminder to worship. Psalms like these can help create your own framework for worshipping God: Psalms 19, 47, 66, 100, 103, 104, or 145. To help you memorize, print a portable copy of these psalms from a Bible study Web site such as BibleGateway.com.

WHAT THE BIBLE SAYS ABOUT WORSHIP

CHAPTER 2
THE FOCUS OF OUR WORSHIP

God gets a lot of competition for my worship. I wish that weren't the case, but it's true. Rather than keeping my thoughts focused on Him, I find myself worshipping my possessions, money, and my job. And as a single guy, there are times when I'm busy worshipping my latest love interest. No, I don't sing praise songs or lift my hands toward them like I do at church, but they do consume my thoughts and receive the bulk of my time and energy. It doesn't take much for these things to take first priority in my life—instead of God.

■ Terry, age 32, Florida ■

WHAT THE BIBLE SAYS ABOUT WORSHIP

WORSHIP THE ONE AND ONLY GOD

■ Jesus answered, "It is written: 'Worship the Lord your God and serve him only.'"

LUKE 4:8 NIV

■ "I am the LORD; that is my name!
I will not give my glory to another
    or my praise to idols."

ISAIAH 42:8 NIV

■ All creation, come praise the name
    of the LORD. Praise his name alone.
The glory of God is greater than heaven
    and earth.

PSALM 148:13 CEV

WHAT THE BIBLE SAYS ABOUT WORSHIP

■ At the time when the LORD had made his solemn agreement with the people of Israel, he told them: Do not worship any other gods! Do not bow down to them or offer them a sacrifice. Worship only me! I am the one who rescued you from Egypt with my mighty power. Bow down to me and offer sacrifices. Never worship any other god, always obey my laws and teachings, and remember the solemn agreement between us.

I will say it again: Do not worship any god except me. I am the LORD your God, and I will rescue you from all your enemies.

2 KINGS 17:35–39 CEV

WHAT THE BIBLE SAYS ABOUT WORSHIP

- The idols of the nations are silver and gold, made by the hands of men. They have mouths, but cannot speak, eyes, but they cannot see; they have ears, but cannot hear, nor is there breath in their mouths. Those who make them will be like them, and so will all who trust in them.... Praise be to the LORD from Zion, to him who dwells in Jerusalem. Praise the LORD.

   PSALM 135:15–18, 21 NIV

- "For who is God besides the LORD?
  And who is the Rock except our God?"

   2 SAMUEL 22:32 NIV

- Is there any god like GOD?
  Are we not at bedrock?

   PSALM 18:31 MSG

WHAT THE BIBLE SAYS ABOUT WORSHIP

- "Who among the gods is like you, O Lord?
    Who is like you—
    majestic in holiness,
    awesome in glory,
    working wonders?"

    EXODUS 15:11 NIV

- With every bone in my body I will praise him:
    "Lord, who can compare with you?
    Who else rescues the helpless
        from the strong?
    Who else protects the helpless and poor
        from those who rob them?"

    PSALM 35:10 NLT

- "O Lord, God of Israel, there is no God like you in heaven above or on earth below—you who keep your covenant of love with your servants who continue wholeheartedly in your way."

    1 KINGS 8:23 NIV

WHAT THE BIBLE SAYS ABOUT WORSHIP

- "Then people all over the earth will know that the Lord alone is God and there is no other."

  1 Kings 8:60 NLT

- No pagan god is like you, O Lord.
  None can do what you do!

  Psalm 86:8 NLT

- He then went back to the Holy Man, he and his entourage, stood before him, and said, "I now know beyond a shadow of a doubt that there is no God anywhere on earth other than the God of Israel. In gratitude let me give you a gift."

  2 Kings 5:15 MSG

- "You shall have no other gods before Me."

  Exodus 20:3 NASB

WHAT THE BIBLE SAYS ABOUT WORSHIP

- "You must worship no other gods, for the Lord, whose very name is Jealous, is a God who is jealous about his relationship with you."

  Exodus 34:14 NLT

- Hezekiah prayed before the Lord and said, "O Lord, the God of Israel, who are enthroned above the cherubim, You are the God, You alone, of all the kingdoms of the earth. You have made heaven and earth."

  2 Kings 19:15 NASB

WHAT THE BIBLE SAYS ABOUT WORSHIP

■ "This is what the Lord says—
>> Israel's King and Redeemer,
>> the Lord Almighty:
> I am the first and I am the last;
>> apart from me there is no God."
>
> ISAIAH 44:6 NIV

WHAT THE BIBLE SAYS ABOUT WORSHIP

WORSHIP THE GREAT ONE

- "How great you are, O Sovereign LORD! There is no one like you, and there is no God but you, as we have heard with our own ears."

  2 SAMUEL 7:22 NIV

- "Great and marvelous are your works,
     O Lord God, the Almighty.
  Just and true are your ways,
     O King of the nations.
  Who will not fear you, Lord,
     and glorify your name?
  For you alone are holy.
  All nations will come and worship before you,
     for your righteous deeds have been revealed."

  REVELATION 15:3-4 NLT

WHAT THE BIBLE SAYS ABOUT WORSHIP

■ I will exalt you, my God the King;
> I will praise your name for ever and ever.
Every day I will praise you
> and extol your name for ever and ever.
Great is the LORD and most worthy of praise;
> his greatness no one can fathom.

PSALM 145:1–3 NIV

■ I will remember the deeds of the LORD;
> yes, I will remember your wonders of old.
I will ponder all your work,
> and meditate on your mighty deeds....
You are the God who works wonders;
> you have made known your might among the peoples.
You with your arm redeemed your people,
> the children of Jacob and Joseph.

PSALM 77:11–12, 14–15 ESV

WHAT THE BIBLE SAYS ABOUT WORSHIP

- Lord, there is no one like you!
  For you are great, and your name is full
      of power.

  JEREMIAH 10:6 NLT

- For the Lord your God is God of gods and Lord of lords, the great God, mighty and awesome, who shows no partiality and accepts no bribes.

  DEUTERONOMY 10:17 NIV

- How awesome is the Lord Most High, the great King over all the earth!

  PSALM 47:2 NIV

- "Yours, O Lord, is the greatness and the power and the glory and the victory and the majesty, indeed everything that is in the heavens and the earth; Yours is the dominion, O Lord, and You exalt Yourself as head over all."

  1 CHRONICLES 29:11 NASB

- Oh, the depth of the riches of the wisdom
    and knowledge of God!
  How unsearchable his judgments,
    and his paths beyond tracing out!
  "Who has known the mind of the Lord?
  Or who has been his counselor?"

  ROMANS 11:33–34 NIV

- "Who has ever given to God,
    that God should repay him?"
  For from him and through him and to him
    are all things.
  To him be the glory forever! Amen.

  ROMANS 11:35–36 NIV

- Splendor and majesty are before him;
  strength and joy in his dwelling place.

  1 CHRONICLES 16:27 NIV

WHAT THE BIBLE SAYS ABOUT WORSHIP

WORSHIP THE HOLY ONE

■ "Do not come any closer," God said. "Take off your sandals, for the place where you are standing is holy ground."

EXODUS 3:5 NIV

■ Moses then said to Aaron, "This is what the LORD spoke of when he said:
>   'Among those who approach me
>   I will show myself holy;
>   in the sight of all the people
>   I will be honored.' "

LEVITICUS 10:3 NIV

■ Our LORD and our God, we praise you and kneel down to worship you, the God of holiness!

PSALM 99:5 CEV

WHAT THE BIBLE SAYS ABOUT WORSHIP

- To the Lord I cry aloud,
  and he answers me from his holy hill.

  PSALM 3:4 NIV

- O God! Your way is holy!
  No god is great like God!

  PSALM 77:13 MSG

- Ascribe to the Lord the glory due to
  His name;
  Worship the Lord in holy array.

  PSALM 29:2 NASB

- Yet you are enthroned as the Holy One;
  you are the praise of Israel.

  PSALM 22:3 NIV

WHAT THE BIBLE SAYS ABOUT WORSHIP

WORSHIP THE CREATOR OF EVERYTHING

- "Ah Lord G<small>OD</small>! Behold, You have made the heavens and the earth by Your great power and by Your outstretched arm! Nothing is too difficult for You."

  J<small>EREMIAH</small> 32:17 <small>NASB</small>

- "Fear God," he shouted. "Give glory to him. For the time has come when he will sit as judge. Worship him who made the heavens, the earth, the sea, and all the springs of water."

  R<small>EVELATION</small> 14:7 <small>NLT</small>

- Know that the L<small>ORD</small> is God. It is he who made us, and we are his; we are his people, the sheep of his pasture.

  P<small>SALM</small> 100:3 <small>NIV</small>

WHAT THE BIBLE SAYS ABOUT WORSHIP

- Blessed be the LORD God of Israel, that made heaven and earth, who hath given to David the king a wise son, endued with prudence and understanding, that might build an house for the LORD, and an house for his kingdom.

    2 CHRONICLES 2:12 KJV

- For every house is built by someone, but God is the builder of everything.

    HEBREWS 3:4 NIV

- "Stand up and praise the LORD your God, who is from everlasting to everlasting."

    "Blessed be your glorious name, and may it be exalted above all blessing and praise. You alone are the LORD. You made the heavens, even the highest heavens, and all their starry host, the earth and all that is on it, the seas and all that is in them. You give life to everything, and the multitudes of heaven worship you."

    NEHEMIAH 9:5–6 NIV

WHAT THE BIBLE SAYS ABOUT WORSHIP

■ The Lord merely spoke,
>   and the heavens were created.
> He breathed the word,
>   and all the stars were born.
> He assigned the sea its boundaries
>   and locked the oceans in vast reservoirs.
> Let the whole world fear the Lord,
>   and let everyone stand in awe of him.
> For when he spoke, the world began!
> It appeared at his command.

PSALM 33:6–9 NLT

■ God alone stretched out the sky, stepped on the sea, and set the stars in place—the Big Dipper and Orion, the Pleiades and the stars in the southern sky.

Of all the miracles God works, we cannot understand a one.

JOB 9:8–10 CEV

WHAT THE BIBLE SAYS ABOUT WORSHIP

- Let all that I am praise the LORD.
  O LORD my God, how great you are!
  You are robed with honor and majesty.
  You are dressed in a robe of light.
  You stretch out the starry curtain of
      the heavens; you lay out the rafters of
      your home in the rain clouds.
  You make the clouds your chariot;
      you ride upon the wings of the wind.
  The winds are your messengers;
      flames of fire are your servants....
  O LORD, what a variety of things you have
      made!
  In wisdom you have made them all.

  PSALM 104:1–4, 24 NLT

- Lord, through all the generations
    you have been our home!
  Before the mountains were born,
    before you gave birth to the earth
    and the world, from beginning to end,
    you are God.

  PSALM 90:1–2 NLT

- When I consider your heavens, the work of your fingers, the moon and the stars, which you have set in place, what is man that you are mindful of him, the son of man that you care for him? You made him a little lower than the heavenly beings and crowned him with glory and honor.

  PSALM 8:3–5 NIV

WHAT THE BIBLE SAYS ABOUT WORSHIP

- For by Him all things were created, both in the heavens and on earth, visible and invisible, whether thrones or dominions or rulers or authorities—all things have been created through Him and for Him.

    He is before all things, and in Him all things hold together.

    COLOSSIANS 1:16–17 NASB

- How many are your works, O LORD!
    In wisdom you made them all; the earth is full of your creatures.

    PSALM 104:24 NIV

WHAT THE BIBLE SAYS ABOUT WORSHIP

WORSHIP THE RULER OF ALL

- For God is the King of all the earth;
  sing to him a psalm of praise.

  PSALM 47:7 NIV

- The LORD reigns, he is robed in majesty;
     the LORD is robed in majesty
     and is armed with strength.
  The world is firmly established;
     it cannot be moved.
  Your throne was established long ago;
     you are from all eternity.

  PSALM 93:1–2 NIV

- Make them realize that you
     are the LORD Most High,
     the only ruler of earth!

  PSALM 83:18 CEV

WHAT THE BIBLE SAYS ABOUT WORSHIP

- I know that the LORD is great, that our Lord is greater than all gods. The LORD does whatever pleases him, in the heavens and on the earth, in the seas and all their depths. He makes clouds rise from the ends of the earth; he sends lightning with the rain and brings out the wind from his storehouses.

    PSALM 135:5–7 NIV

- The earth is the LORD's and the fullness thereof, the world and those who dwell therein.

    PSALM 24:1 ESV

- To the LORD your God belong the heavens, even the highest heavens, the earth and everything in it.

    DEUTERONOMY 10:14 NIV

WHAT THE BIBLE SAYS ABOUT WORSHIP

■ "He is the God who made the world and everything in it. Since he is Lord of heaven and earth, he doesn't live in man-made temples, and human hands can't serve his needs—for he has no needs. He himself gives life and breath to everything, and he satisfies every need. From one man he created all the nations throughout the whole earth. He decided beforehand when they should rise and fall, and he determined their boundaries.

"His purpose was for the nations to seek after God and perhaps feel their way toward him and find him—though he is not far from any one of us. For in him we live and move and exist. As some of your own poets have said, 'We are his offspring.'"

Acts 17:24–28 NLT

WHAT THE BIBLE SAYS ABOUT WORSHIP

- "Yours, O Lord, is the greatness and the power and the glory and the majesty and the splendor, for everything in heaven and earth is yours. Yours, O Lord, is the kingdom; you are exalted as head over all. Wealth and honor come from you; you are the ruler of all things. In your hands are strength and power to exalt and give strength to all."

    1 Chronicles 29:11–12 niv

- God will be king over all the earth, one God and only one. What a Day that will be!

    Zechariah 14:9 msg

WHAT THE BIBLE SAYS ABOUT WORSHIP

WORSHIP THE LIVING GOD

- But God is the real thing—
  the living God, the eternal King.
  When he's angry, Earth shakes.
  Yes, and the godless nations quake.

  JEREMIAH 10:10 MSG

- My soul longs, yes, faints for the courts of the LORD; my heart and flesh sing for joy to the living God.

  PSALM 84:2 ESV

- "For he is the living God,
  and he will endure forever.
  His kingdom will never be destroyed,
  and his rule will never end."

  DANIEL 6:26 NLT

WHAT THE BIBLE SAYS ABOUT WORSHIP

■ My soul thirsts for God, for the living God. When can I go and meet with God?

PSALM 42:2 NIV

■ "We have come to bring you the Good News that you should turn from these worthless things and turn to the living God, who made heaven and earth, the sea, and everything in them."

ACTS 14:15 NLT

■ But Christ was sinless, and he offered himself as an eternal and spiritual sacrifice to God. That's why his blood is much more powerful and makes our consciences clear. Now we can serve the living God and no longer do things that lead to death.

HEBREWS 9:14 CEV

WHAT THE BIBLE SAYS ABOUT WORSHIP

WORSHIP THE APPROACHABLE FATHER

- The Spirit and the bride say, "Come!" And let him who hears say, "Come!" Whoever is thirsty, let him come; and whoever wishes, let him take the free gift of the water of life.

    REVELATION 22:17 NIV

- Let us then approach the throne of grace with confidence, so that we may receive mercy and find grace to help us in our time of need.

    HEBREWS 4:16 NIV

- For there is only one God and one Mediator who can reconcile God and humanity—the man Christ Jesus.

    1 TIMOTHY 2:5 NLT

WHAT THE BIBLE SAYS ABOUT WORSHIP

- God, high above, sees far below; no matter the distance, he knows everything about us.

  PSALM 138:6 MSG

- Pay close attention! Come to me and live. I will promise you the eternal love and loyalty that I promised David.

  ISAIAH 55:3 CEV

- "And you, my son Solomon, acknowledge the God of your father, and serve him with wholehearted devotion and with a willing mind, for the Lord searches every heart and understands every motive behind the thoughts. If you seek him, he will be found by you; but if you forsake him, he will reject you forever."

  1 CHRONICLES 28:9 NIV

WHAT THE BIBLE SAYS ABOUT WORSHIP

- Come near to God and he will come near to you. Wash your hands, you sinners, and purify your hearts, you double-minded.

    JAMES 4:8 NIV

- But now in Christ Jesus you who once were far off have been brought near by the blood of Christ.

    EPHESIANS 2:13 NKJV

- And he came and preached peace to you who were far off and peace to those who were near. For through him we both have access in one Spirit to the Father.

    EPHESIANS 2:17–18 ESV

ONE MOMENT AT A TIME
GOD FIRST

- **Identify your idols.** Few people reading this book are likely to erect and worship statues in their home. Still, idols come in all shapes and forms. Anything that you make sacrifices for, anything that commands your time and attention, or anything that takes center stage in your heart could be considered an idol. Take a few moments and contemplate which things in your life divert your attention from God. For many, this might include jobs, possessions, 401(k) accounts, hobbies, or relationships. What is it for you?

- **Create worship prompters.** Keep your eyes focused on Christ by reminding yourself to worship God. Create a reminder you'll see or hear throughout the day to prompt you to take a few moments to worship God. Ideas include: a note taped to your computer monitor or bathroom mirror, a daily reminder on your PDA, or an alarm set on your watch.

- **Make room in your schedule.** Adding worship to your already crowded day can be difficult, especially if it is a new exercise. Try treating it like an exercise program and begin with small steps. Begin with five minutes of worship. As you become more comfortable, expand it to ten minutes, then fifteen.

WHAT THE BIBLE SAYS ABOUT WORSHIP

CHAPTER 3
WHO SHOULD WORSHIP GOD

The book of Psalms ranked as my least favorite Bible book for a long time. Since I'm just not a very emotional person, I've always had trouble relating to the unrestrained prayers found in the book. Usually, when choosing a part of the Bible to read, I'd just skip over this one. Our pastor recently preached through some psalms, and I realized that as I've neglected this portion of God's Word, I've neglected to worship. The Bible makes it clear that everyone is to worship—even private, and often stoic, people like me. The way I worship might look different than it would for someone with a different personality, but God deserves my worship, and I know I need to grow in this area. It hasn't gotten magically easy, but I'm trying.

■ Buck, age 50, Colorado ■

WHAT THE BIBLE SAYS ABOUT WORSHIP

WORSHIP IS DUE FROM EVERYONE

- Shout to the LORD, all the earth;
  break out in praise and sing for joy!

  PSALM 98:4 NLT

- May the peoples praise you, O God;
  may all the peoples praise you.

  PSALM 67:5 NIV

- Sing to God, you kingdoms of the earth.
  Sing praises to the Lord.

  PSALM 68:32 NLT

- I will perpetuate your memory through all generations; therefore the nations will praise you for ever and ever.

  PSALM 45:17 NIV

WHAT THE BIBLE SAYS ABOUT WORSHIP

- The LORD sits in majesty in Jerusalem,
    exalted above all the nations.
  Let them praise your great and
    awesome name.
  Your name is holy!

  PSALM 99:2–3 NLT

- Sing to the LORD a new song,
  And His praise from the ends of the earth,
  You who go down to the sea,
    and all that is in it,
  You coastlands and you inhabitants of them!
  Let the wilderness and its cities lift up
    their voice,
  The villages that Kedar inhabits.
  Let the inhabitants of Sela sing,
  Let them shout from the top of
    the mountains.

  ISAIAH 42:10–11 NKJV

WHAT THE BIBLE SAYS ABOUT WORSHIP

- "All the earth bows down to you;
    they sing praise to you,
    they sing praise to your name."

    PSALM 66:4 NIV

- May all the kings of the earth praise you,
O LORD, when they hear the words of your mouth.
    May they sing of the ways of the LORD,
for the glory of the LORD is great.

    PSALM 138:4–5 NIV

- Then I heard every creature in heaven and on earth and under the earth and on the sea, and all that is in them, singing:
    "To him who sits on the throne and to the Lamb be praise and honor and glory and power, for ever and ever!"

    REVELATION 5:13 NIV

WHAT THE BIBLE SAYS ABOUT WORSHIP

- Praise the Lord, all nations!
    Extol him, all peoples!

    PSALM 117:1 ESV

- Therefore God has highly exalted him and bestowed on him the name that is above every name, so that at the name of Jesus every knee should bow, in heaven and on earth and under the earth, and every tongue confess that Jesus Christ is Lord, to the glory of God the Father.

    PHILIPPIANS 2:9–11 ESV

WHAT THE BIBLE SAYS ABOUT WORSHIP

WORSHIP IS OFFERED BY CREATION

■ The heavens declare the glory of God;
the skies proclaim the work of his hands.

PSALM 19:1 NIV

■ Praise the LORD, everything he has created,
everything in all his kingdom.
Let all that I am praise the LORD.

PSALM 103:22 NLT

■ Sing, O heavens, for the LORD has done this
wondrous thing.
Shout for joy, O depths of the earth!
Break into song, O mountains and forests
and every tree!
For the LORD has redeemed Jacob
and is glorified in Israel.

ISAIAH 44:23 NLT

WHAT THE BIBLE SAYS ABOUT WORSHIP

■ "You will go out in joy and be led forth
in peace; the mountains and hills
will burst into song before you,
and all the trees of the field will clap
their hands."

ISAIAH 55:12 NIV

■ Let the heavens be glad, and the earth
    rejoice!
Let the sea and everything in it shout his
    praise!
Let the fields and their crops burst out
    with joy!
Let the trees of the forest rustle with praise
    before the LORD, for he is coming!
He is coming to judge the earth.
He will judge the world with justice,
    and the nations with his truth.

PSALM 96:11–13 NLT

WHAT THE BIBLE SAYS ABOUT WORSHIP

■ Praise him, sun and moon!
Praise him, all you twinkling stars!
Praise him, skies above!
Praise him, vapors high above the clouds!
Let every created thing give praise to the
    Lord, for he issued his command, and
    they came into being.
He set them in place forever and ever.
His decree will never be revoked.
Praise the Lord from the earth,
    you creatures of the ocean depths,
    fire and hail, snow and clouds,
    wind and weather that obey him,
    mountains and all hills,
    fruit trees and all cedars,
    wild animals and all livestock,
    small scurrying animals and birds.

Psalm 148:3–10 NLT

WHAT THE BIBLE SAYS ABOUT WORSHIP

- Let the sea and everything in it shout
    his praise!
  Let the earth and all living things join in.
  Let the rivers clap their hands in glee!
  Let the hills sing out their songs of joy.

  PSALM 98:7–8 NLT

WHAT THE BIBLE SAYS ABOUT WORSHIP

WORSHIP IS GIVEN BY ANGELS

■ Praise the Lord, you his angels,
> you mighty ones who do his bidding,
> who obey his word.
> Praise the Lord, all his heavenly hosts,
> you his servants who do his will.

>> Psalm 103:20–21 niv

■ Praise the Lord! Praise the Lord from the heavens; praise him in the heights!
> Praise him, all his angels; praise him, all his hosts!

>> Psalm 148:1–2 esv

■ And suddenly there was with the angel a multitude of the heavenly host praising God and saying, "Glory to God in the highest!"

>> Luke 2:13–14 esv

WHAT THE BIBLE SAYS ABOUT WORSHIP

- "Where were you when I laid the earth's foundation?
Tell me, if you understand....
    while the morning stars sang together
    and all the angels shouted for joy?"

    JOB 38:4, 7 NIV

- I looked again. I heard a company of Angels around the Throne, the Animals, and the Elders—ten thousand times ten thousand their number, thousand after thousand after thousand in full song: The slain Lamb is worthy! Take the power, the wealth, the wisdom, the strength! Take the honor, the glory, the blessing!

    REVELATION 5:11–12 MSG

- When he presents his honored Son to the world, he says, "All angels must worship him."

    HEBREWS 1:6 MSG

WHAT THE BIBLE SAYS ABOUT WORSHIP

■ All the angels were standing around the throne and around the elders and the four living creatures. They fell down on their faces before the throne and worshiped God.

REVELATION 7:11 NIV

WHAT THE BIBLE SAYS ABOUT WORSHIP

WORSHIP IS ENCOURAGED FROM CHILDREN

- "Do you hear what these children are
         saying?" they asked him.
    "Yes," replied Jesus, "have you never read,
    " 'From the lips of children and infants
         you have ordained praise'?"

    MATTHEW 21:16 NIV

- Young men and maidens,
         old men and children.
    Let them praise the name of the LORD,
         for his name alone is exalted;
         his splendor is above the earth
         and the heavens.

    PSALM 148:12–13 NIV

WHAT THE BIBLE SAYS ABOUT WORSHIP

■ Lord, our Lord, how majestic is your name in
   all the earth!
You have set your glory above the heavens.
From the lips of children and infants
   you have ordained praise because of
   your enemies, to silence the foe
   and the avenger.

Psalm 8:1–2 NIV

WORSHIP IS PRESENTED BY HIS PEOPLE

- Praise the Lord.
  Praise the name of the Lord;
  > praise him, you servants of the Lord,
  > you who minister in the house of the
  > Lord, in the courts of the house of
  > our God.

  PSALM 135:1–2 NIV

- Sing to the Lord, you saints of his;
  > praise his holy name.

  PSALM 30:4 NIV

- Sing joyfully to the Lord, you righteous;
  > it is fitting for the upright to praise him.

  PSALM 33:1 NIV

- All you have made will praise you,
  > O Lord; your saints will extol you.

  PSALM 145:10 NIV

WHAT THE BIBLE SAYS ABOUT WORSHIP

- Surely the righteous will praise your name
  and the upright will live before you.

  PSALM 140:13 NIV

- Rejoice in the LORD, you who are righteous,
  and praise his holy name.

  PSALM 97:12 NIV

- Praise the LORD, all you servants of the
  LORD who minister by night in the house
  of the LORD.

  Lift up your hands in the sanctuary
  and praise the LORD.

  PSALM 134:1–2 NIV

- "Blessed be GOD who has delivered you from
  the power of Egypt and Pharaoh, who has
  delivered his people from the oppression of
  Egypt."

  EXODUS 18:10 MSG

WHAT THE BIBLE SAYS ABOUT WORSHIP

- "And blessed be God, your God, who took such a liking to you and made you king. Clearly, God's love for Israel is behind this, making you king to keep a just order and nurture a God-pleasing people."

  1 Kings 10:9 msg

- Join with me in praising the wonderful name of the Lord our God.

  The Lord is a mighty rock, and he never does wrong.

  God can always be trusted to bring justice.

  Deuteronomy 32:3–4 cev

- Sing to him, sing praise to him; tell of all his wonderful acts. . . .

  For great is the Lord and most worthy of praise; he is to be feared above all gods.

  1 Chronicles 16:9, 25 niv

ONE MOMENT AT A TIME
CHOOSING TO WORSHIP

■ **Worship without singing.** While many people equate worship with singing, the two are not exclusively linked. Praise God with a reverent spirit, the words you speak, and the attitudes you carry with you throughout the day. You can find a way to worship God in every activity throughout your day—without singing a single note.

- **Disregard your feelings.** The Bible encourages us to worship at all times—whether we feel like it or not. Make it a priority to spend time worshipping God regularly, no matter what emotions you're feeling.

- **Read a story from the Gospels.** Read an episode from the life of Christ in Matthew, Mark, Luke, or John. As you read the story, look for attributes of God you find in Christ. Pause and worship God as you encounter each one.

CHAPTER 4
HOW WE SHOULD WORSHIP

While no one has ever told me this, I think I've figured out that worship is an acquired skill. Yes, certain aspects of worship come pretty easily, but others require work. I've realized that I need to constantly pursue improving in those areas, and even then, I'll probably never perfect them. Learning to keep an attitude of reverence in all things is especially difficult for me because I'm pretty self-absorbed. Maintaining a grateful spirit never comes easily for me because I'm a "glass half-empty" person. I have noticed, though, that as I think about it and work on it, God slowly changes me.

■ Tanya, age 32, Oklahoma ■

WHAT THE BIBLE SAYS ABOUT WORSHIP

WORSHIP WITH CONSTANT PRAISE

- Look to the Lord and his strength;
  seek his face always.

  1 Chronicles 16:11 niv

- What joy for those who can live in your house, always singing your praises.

  Psalm 84:4 nlt

- Rejoice in hope, be patient in tribulation,
  be constant in prayer.

  Romans 12:12 esv

- I will sing to the Lord as long as I live.
  I will praise my God to my last breath!

  Psalm 104:33 nlt

- My mouth is filled with your praise,
  declaring your splendor all day long.

  Psalm 71:8 niv

WHAT THE BIBLE SAYS ABOUT WORSHIP

■ But as for me, I will always proclaim what God has done; I will sing praises to the God of Jacob.

PSALM 75:9 NLT

■ The LORD will save me, and we will sing with stringed instruments all the days of our lives in the temple of the LORD.

ISAIAH 38:20 NIV

■ Then my tongue shall tell of your righteousness and of your praise all the day long.

PSALM 35:28 ESV

■ Because he turned his ear to me,
    I will call on him as long as I live.

PSALM 116:2 NIV

WHAT THE BIBLE SAYS ABOUT WORSHIP

- I will praise the LORD all my life;
    I will sing praise to my God as long
    as I live.

    PSALM 146:2 NIV

- In God we boast all day long,
    And praise Your name forever.

    PSALM 44:8 NKJV

WHAT THE BIBLE SAYS ABOUT WORSHIP

WORSHIP WITH GREAT JOY

- Shout for joy, O heavens! And rejoice,
    O earth!
  Break forth into joyful shouting,
    O mountains!
  For the Lord has comforted His people
  And will have compassion on His afflicted.

  ISAIAH 49:13 NASB

- This is the day the Lord has made;
    let us rejoice and be glad in it.

  PSALM 118:24 NIV

- I will shout for joy and sing your praises,
  for you have ransomed me.

  PSALM 71:23 NLT

WHAT THE BIBLE SAYS ABOUT WORSHIP

- Sing praises to God and to his name!
  Sing loud praises to him who rides
     the clouds.
  His name is the L%%ORD%%—rejoice in his
     presence!

  P%%SALM%% 68:4 NLT

- Then will I go to the altar of God,
     to God, my joy and my delight.
  I will praise you with the harp,
     O God, my God.

  P%%SALM%% 43:4 NIV

- You have filled my heart with greater joy
  than when their grain and new wine abound.
     I will lie down and sleep in peace,
  for you alone, O L%%ORD%%, make me dwell in
  safety.

  P%%SALM%% 4:7–8 NIV

WHAT THE BIBLE SAYS ABOUT WORSHIP

■ I will be glad and rejoice in you;
>   I will sing praise to your name,
>   O Most High.

>   PSALM 9:2 NIV

WHAT THE BIBLE SAYS ABOUT WORSHIP

WORSHIP WITH REVERENT FEAR

- You are the most fearsome of all who live in heaven; all the others fear and greatly honor you.

   PSALM 89:7 CEV

- You alone are to be feared. Who can stand before you when you are angry?

   PSALM 76:7 NIV

- "Look now; I myself am he!
  There is no other god but me!
  I am the one who kills and gives life;
   I am the one who wounds and heals;
   no one can be rescued from my powerful hand!"

   DEUTERONOMY 32:39 NLT

WHAT THE BIBLE SAYS ABOUT WORSHIP

- "Have you no respect for me?
  Why don't you tremble in my presence?
  I, the LORD, define the ocean's sandy shoreline
      as an everlasting boundary that
      the waters cannot cross.
  The waves may toss and roar,
      but they can never pass the boundaries
      I set."

  JEREMIAH 5:22 NLT

- Who should not revere you,
      O King of the nations?
  This is your due.
  Among all the wise men of the nations
      and in all their kingdoms,
      there is no one like you.

  JEREMIAH 10:7 NIV

WHAT THE BIBLE SAYS ABOUT WORSHIP

- For all the gods of the nations are idols,
    but the LORD made the heavens.
  Splendor and majesty are before him;
    strength and glory are in his sanctuary.
  Ascribe to the LORD, O families of nations,
    ascribe to the LORD glory and strength....
  Worship the LORD in the splendor of his
    holiness; tremble before him, all the earth.

  PSALM 96:5–7, 9 NIV

WHAT THE BIBLE SAYS ABOUT WORSHIP

WORSHIP WITH GRATEFUL HEARTS

■ So, God's people, shout praise to God,
Give thanks to our Holy God!

Psalm 97:12 msg

■ We give thanks to you, O God, we give thanks, for your Name is near; men tell of your wonderful deeds.

Psalm 75:1 niv

■ Give thanks to the Lord, for he is good; his love endures forever.

1 Chronicles 16:34 niv

■ So thank God for his marvelous love,
for his miracle mercy to the children he loves.

Psalm 107:8 msg

WHAT THE BIBLE SAYS ABOUT WORSHIP

- Devote yourselves to prayer, keeping alert in it with an attitude of thanksgiving.

  COLOSSIANS 4:2 NASB

- David appointed the following Levites to lead the people in worship before the Ark of the LORD—to invoke his blessings, to give thanks, and to praise the LORD, the God of Israel.

  1 CHRONICLES 16:4 NLT

- "Now, our God, we give you thanks, and praise your glorious name."

  1 CHRONICLES 29:13 NIV

WHAT THE BIBLE SAYS ABOUT WORSHIP

■ Enter his gates with thanksgiving and his courts with praise; give thanks to him and praise his name.

PSALM 100:4 NIV

WHAT THE BIBLE SAYS ABOUT WORSHIP

WORSHIP WITH THE SPIRIT'S HELP

- "Yet a time is coming and has now come when the true worshipers will worship the Father in spirit and truth, for they are the kind of worshipers the Father seeks. God is spirit, and his worshipers must worship in spirit and in truth."

    JOHN 4:23–24 NIV

- But you, dear friends, carefully build yourselves up in this most holy faith by praying in the Holy Spirit.

    JUDE 20 MSG

- Pray in the Spirit on all occasions with all kinds of prayers and requests. With this in mind, be alert and always keep on praying for all the saints.

    EPHESIANS 6:18 NIV

- In the same way, the Spirit helps us in our weakness. We do not know what we ought to pray for, but the Spirit himself intercedes for us with groans that words cannot express. And he who searches our hearts knows the mind of the Spirit, because the Spirit intercedes for the saints in accordance with God's will.

  ROMANS 8:26–27 NIV

- Don't you know that you yourselves are God's temple and that God's Spirit lives in you?

  1 CORINTHIANS 3:16 NIV

ONE MOMENT AT A TIME

LEARNING TO WORSHIP

- **Understand reverence.** Look up the word *reverence* in a dictionary. Then see how the word is used in Nehemiah 5:15, Psalm 5:7, Daniel 6:26, Ephesians 5:21, and Hebrews 12:28. What do you learn about reverence? If you went about your next day's required activities with a spirit of reverence, what would look different?

- **Create a poster.** Get a big poster board like a child might use in grade school. Write two or three things on the board that remind you that God is worthy of your praise. Add one or two items each day until your board is full.

- **Ask for help.** The Holy Spirit is your greatest ally in learning to praise God. Ask for His help as you seek to praise God throughout this next week.

WHAT THE BIBLE SAYS ABOUT WORSHIP

CHAPTER 5
WORSHIPPING GOD WITH OUR ACTIONS

As an athlete growing up, I had a lot of coaches. Once, I had a Christian coach who took me under her wing and really impressed on me that every action can be an act of worship—even those done on the court. Developing my God-given gifts is an act of worship. Competing hard and for God's glory is an act of worship. My interaction with teammates and opponents can be an act of worship. I had never thought of it that way before, but it caused me to realize that if athletics can be a form of worship, then anything can.

■ Trinity, age 26, Michigan ■

WHAT THE BIBLE SAYS ABOUT WORSHIP

WORSHIP BY DEVELOPING YOUR GIFTS

- It was he who gave some to be apostles, some to be prophets, some to be evangelists, and some to be pastors and teachers, to prepare God's people for works of service, so that the body of Christ may be built up.

    EPHESIANS 4:11–12 NIV

- There are different kinds of gifts, but the same Spirit. There are different kinds of service, but the same Lord. There are different kinds of working, but the same God works all of them in all men.

    Now to each one the manifestation of the Spirit is given for the common good.

    1 CORINTHIANS 12:4–7 NIV

WHAT THE BIBLE SAYS ABOUT WORSHIP

- Each of you has been blessed with one of God's many wonderful gifts to be used in the service of others. So use your gift well. If you have the gift of speaking, preach God's message. If you have the gift of helping others, do it with the strength that God supplies. Everything should be done in a way that will bring honor to God because of Jesus Christ, who is glorious and powerful forever. Amen.

    1 Peter 4:10–11 cev

- Whether, then, you eat or drink or whatever you do, do all to the glory of God.

    1 Corinthians 10:31 nasb

- Whatever you do, work at it with all your heart, as working for the Lord, not for men.

    Colossians 3:23 niv

- Never give up. Eagerly follow the Holy Spirit and serve the Lord.

    Romans 12:11 cev

WHAT THE BIBLE SAYS ABOUT WORSHIP

■ "This is to my Father's glory, that you bear much fruit, showing yourselves to be my disciples."

JOHN 15:8 NIV

WHAT THE BIBLE SAYS ABOUT WORSHIP

WORSHIP BY LIVING RIGHTEOUSLY

- Do not offer the parts of your body to sin, as instruments of wickedness, but rather offer yourselves to God, as those who have been brought from death to life; and offer the parts of your body to him as instruments of righteousness.

    ROMANS 6:13 NIV

- Therefore, I urge you, brothers, in view of God's mercy, to offer your bodies as living sacrifices, holy and pleasing to God—this is your spiritual act of worship. Do not conform any longer to the pattern of this world, but be transformed by the renewing of your mind. Then you will be able to test and approve what God's will is—his good, pleasing and perfect will.

    ROMANS 12:1–2 NIV

WHAT THE BIBLE SAYS ABOUT WORSHIP

■ And this is my prayer: that your love may abound more and more in knowledge and depth of insight, so that you may be able to discern what is best and may be pure and blameless until the day of Christ, filled with the fruit of righteousness that comes through Jesus Christ—to the glory and praise of God.

PHILIPPIANS 1:9–11 NIV

■ To this end we always pray for you, that our God may make you worthy of his calling and may fulfill every resolve for good and every work of faith by his power, so that the name of our Lord Jesus may be glorified in you, and you in him, according to the grace of our God and the Lord Jesus Christ.

2 THESSALONIANS 1:11–12 ESV

WHAT THE BIBLE SAYS ABOUT WORSHIP

- Do you not know that your body is a temple of the Holy Spirit, who is in you, whom you have received from God? You are not your own; you were bought at a price. Therefore honor God with your body.

    1 CORINTHIANS 6:19–20 NIV

- Who may worship in your sanctuary, LORD?
    Who may enter your presence on your
        holy hill?
    Those who lead blameless lives and do
        what is right, speaking the truth from
        sincere hearts.

    PSALM 15:1–2 NLT

- God "will give to each person according to what he has done." To those who by persistence in doing good seek glory, honor and immortality, he will give eternal life.

    ROMANS 2:6–7 NIV

WHAT THE BIBLE SAYS ABOUT WORSHIP

■ We exhorted each one of you and encouraged you and charged you to walk in a manner worthy of God, who calls you into his own kingdom and glory.

1 THESSALONIANS 2:12 ESV

WHAT THE BIBLE SAYS ABOUT WORSHIP

WORSHIP BY GIVING

- Honor the LORD with your wealth,
  with the firstfruits of all your crops;
  then your barns will be filled to overflowing,
  and your vats will brim over with new wine.

  PROVERBS 3:9–10 NIV

- And now I have it all—and keep getting more! The gifts you sent with Epaphroditus were more than enough, like a sweet-smelling sacrifice roasting on the altar, filling the air with fragrance, pleasing God no end.

  PHILIPPIANS 4:18 MSG

- "Bring your full tithe to the Temple treasury so there will be ample provisions in my Temple. Test me in this and see if I don't open up heaven itself to you and pour out blessings beyond your wildest dreams."

  MALACHI 3:10 MSG

WHAT THE BIBLE SAYS ABOUT WORSHIP

WORSHIP BY CARING FOR THE NEEDY

- But don't forget to help others and to share your possessions with them. This too is like offering a sacrifice that pleases God.

    HEBREWS 13:16 CEV

- "Then the King will say to those on his right, 'Come, you who are blessed by my Father; take your inheritance, the kingdom prepared for you since the creation of the world. For I was hungry and you gave me something to eat, I was thirsty and you gave me something to drink, I was a stranger and you invited me in, I needed clothes and you clothed me, I was sick and you looked after me, I was in prison and you came to visit me.' ...

    "The King will reply, 'I tell you the truth, whatever you did for one of the least of these brothers of mine, you did for me.'"

    MATTHEW 25:34–36, 40 NIV

WHAT THE BIBLE SAYS ABOUT WORSHIP

■ If anyone considers himself religious and yet does not keep a tight rein on his tongue, he deceives himself and his religion is worthless. Religion that God our Father accepts as pure and faultless is this: to look after orphans and widows in their distress and to keep oneself from being polluted by the world.

JAMES 1:26–27 NIV

ONE MOMENT AT A TIME

REACHING OUT

- **Make a list.** Create a list of the gifts, talents, and opportunities God has given you. How could verses like Romans 12:1–2 affect how you develop each of those?

- **Write your own psalm.** While the Bible has 150 psalms that can serve as model prayers, they are not all-inclusive. Write your own prayer and psalm and offer it as a gift of worship to God.

- **Expand your vision.** While it's easy to see that attending church or singing worship choruses can be acts of worship, you may have to work at looking for new ways you can worship God. Seek out new ways to express your worship to God—like reaching out to someone in need, giving of your money, or using your talents to benefit someone else—and you'll find the possibilities are endless.

CHAPTER 6
FORMS OF WORSHIP

We often have visitors at our church who are used to more reserved worship styles. I enjoy watching their wide-eyed responses when some of our young people dance during the service. Sometimes our students will dance alongside someone else who is kneeling or even step over someone who is lying down as they pray before God. We don't hold anything back, so I can understand why they're surprised to see us be so free. We express our worship differently than many do. That doesn't make our worship any better or any worse than someone else's. It just means that we understand that there is more than one appropriate way to worship and give God the glory He deserves.

■ Mariano, age 41, Dominican Republic ■

WHAT THE BIBLE SAYS ABOUT WORSHIP

WORSHIP WITH OTHERS

- I will sacrifice a thank offering to you
  and call on the name of the Lord.
  > I will fulfill my vows to the Lord
  in the presence of all his people,
  in the courts of the house of the Lord—
  in your midst, O Jerusalem.
  > Praise the Lord.

  > > Psalm 116:17–19 niv

- Glorify the Lord with me;
  > let us exalt his name together.

  > > Psalm 34:3 niv

- Praise our God, O peoples,
  > let the sound of his praise be heard.

  > > Psalm 66:8 niv

WHAT THE BIBLE SAYS ABOUT WORSHIP

- Come, let us sing for joy to the Lord;
  let us shout aloud to the Rock of our
  salvation....for he is our God and we
  are the people of his pasture, the flock
  under his care.

  PSALM 95:1, 7 NIV

- I'll tell my good friends, my brothers and
     sisters, all I know about you;
  I'll join them in worship and praise to you.

  HEBREWS 2:12 MSG

- I will declare your name to my brothers;
     in the congregation I will praise you.

  PSALM 22:22 NIV

- Praise God in the great congregation;
     praise the Lord in the assembly of Israel.

  PSALM 68:26 NIV

WHAT THE BIBLE SAYS ABOUT WORSHIP

■ I will give you thanks in the great assembly; among throngs of people I will praise you.

PSALM 35:18 NIV

■ From you comes the theme of my praise in the great assembly; before those who fear you will I fulfill my vows.

PSALM 22:25 NIV

■ "Again, I tell you that if two of you on earth agree about anything you ask for, it will be done for you by my Father in heaven."

MATTHEW 18:19 NIV

WHAT THE BIBLE SAYS ABOUT WORSHIP

WORSHIP WITH SONG

■ He has given me a new song to sing,
a hymn of praise to our God.
Many will see what he has done and
be amazed.
They will put their trust in the Lord.

PSALM 40:3 NLT

■ Serve the Lord with gladness!
Come into his presence with singing!

PSALM 100:2 ESV

■ Shout praises to the Lord!
Sing him a new song of praise when
his loyal people meet.

PSALM 149:1 CEV

■ Sing to the Lord a new song;
sing to the Lord, all the earth.

PSALM 96:1 NIV

WHAT THE BIBLE SAYS ABOUT WORSHIP

- Sing praises to God, sing praises!
  Sing praises to our King, sing praises!

  PSALM 47:6 ESV

- Is any one of you in trouble? He should pray.
  Is anyone happy? Let him sing songs of praise.

  JAMES 5:13 NIV

- I will give thanks to you, O Lord,
     among the peoples;
  I will sing praises to you among the nations.

  PSALM 57:9 ESV

- I will sing to the LORD,
     for he has been good to me.

  PSALM 13:6 NIV

- Therefore I will praise you among the nations,
  O LORD; I will sing praises to your name.

  PSALM 18:49 NIV

WHAT THE BIBLE SAYS ABOUT WORSHIP

- "Listen, you kings! Pay attention,
  you mighty rulers!
  For I will sing to the Lord.
  I will make music to the Lord,
  the God of Israel."

  JUDGES 5:3 NLT

- "Therefore I will give thanks to You,
  O Lord, among the nations,
  And I will sing praises to Your name."

  2 SAMUEL 22:50 NASB

- Then Moses and the Israelites sang this song to the Lord:
  "I will sing to the Lord,
  for he is highly exalted.
  The horse and its rider
  he has hurled into the sea."

  EXODUS 15:1 NIV

WHAT THE BIBLE SAYS ABOUT WORSHIP

WORSHIP WITH MUSICAL INSTRUMENTS

- Tell everyone on this earth to sing happy
     songs in praise of the Lord.
  Make music for him on harps.
  Play beautiful melodies!

  PSALM 98:4–5 CEV

- Praise the Lord, for the Lord is good;
  celebrate his lovely name with music.

  PSALM 135:3 NLT

- My heart is steadfast, O God,
     my heart is steadfast;
     I will sing and make music.

  PSALM 57:7 NIV

WHAT THE BIBLE SAYS ABOUT WORSHIP

■ Then my head will be exalted above the enemies who surround me; at his tabernacle will I sacrifice with shouts of joy; I will sing and make music to the LORD.

PSALM 27:6 NIV

■ Shout praises to the LORD!
Praise God in his temple.
Praise him in heaven, his mighty fortress.
Praise our God!
His deeds are wonderful,
    too marvelous to describe.
Praise God with trumpets and
    all kinds of harps.
Praise him with tambourines and dancing,
    with stringed instruments
    and woodwinds.
Praise God with cymbals, with clashing cymbals.
Let every living creature praise the LORD.
Shout praises to the LORD!

PSALM 150:1–6 CEV

WHAT THE BIBLE SAYS ABOUT WORSHIP

- David and the whole house of Israel were celebrating with all their might before the LORD, with songs and with harps, lyres, tambourines, sistrums and cymbals.

  2 SAMUEL 6:5 NIV

- Praise the LORD with the harp;
    make music to him on the
    ten-stringed lyre.
  Sing to him a new song;
    play skillfully, and shout for joy.

  PSALM 33:2–3 NIV

WHAT THE BIBLE SAYS ABOUT WORSHIP

WORSHIP WITH WHAT YOU SAY

- May the words of my mouth and
    the meditation of my heart
    be pleasing in your sight,
    O L ORD, my Rock and my Redeemer.

    P SALM 19:14 NIV

- I will praise the L ORD at all times.
  I will constantly speak his praises.

    P SALM 34:1 NLT

- With my mouth I will greatly extol the L ORD;
    in the great throng I will praise him.
  For he stands at the right hand of the needy
    one, to save his life from those who
    condemn him.

    P SALM 109:30–31 NIV

WHAT THE BIBLE SAYS ABOUT WORSHIP

- O Lord, open my lips, and my mouth will declare your praise.

  PSALM 51:15 NIV

- My soul will be satisfied as with fat and rich food, and my mouth will praise you with joyful lips.

  PSALM 63:5 ESV

- Don't repay evil for evil. Don't retaliate with insults when people insult you. Instead, pay them back with a blessing. That is what God has called you to do, and he will bless you for it. For the Scriptures say, "If you want to enjoy life and see many happy days, keep your tongue from speaking evil and your lips from telling lies. Turn away from evil and do good. Search for peace, and work to maintain it."

  1 PETER 3:9–11 NLT

WHAT THE BIBLE SAYS ABOUT WORSHIP

- Do not let any unwholesome talk come out of your mouths, but only what is helpful for building others up according to their needs, that it may benefit those who listen.

  EPHESIANS 4:29 NIV

- All of us do many wrong things. But if you can control your tongue, you are mature and able to control your whole body.... My dear friends, with our tongues we speak both praises and curses. We praise our Lord and Father, and we curse people who were created to be like God, and this isn't right.

  JAMES 3:2, 9–10 CEV

WHAT THE BIBLE SAYS ABOUT WORSHIP

WORSHIP WITH REVERENT POSTURE

- Then David said to the whole assembly, "Praise the Lord your God." So they all praised the Lord, the God of their fathers; they bowed low and fell prostrate before the Lord and the king.

    1 Chronicles 29:20 niv

- Come, let us worship and bow down. Let us kneel before the Lord our maker.

    Psalm 95:6 nlt

- My response is to get down on my knees before the Father, this magnificent Father who parcels out all heaven and earth.

    Ephesians 3:14–15 msg

WHAT THE BIBLE SAYS ABOUT WORSHIP

- And Hezekiah the king and the officials commanded the Levites to sing praises to the LORD with the words of David and of Asaph the seer. And they sang praises with gladness, and they bowed down and worshiped.

    2 CHRONICLES 29:30 ESV

- I will praise you as long as I live,
  and in your name I will lift up my hands.

    PSALM 63:4 NIV

- I lift up my hands to your commands, which I love, and I meditate on your decrees.

    PSALM 119:48 NIV

- Lift up your hands in the sanctuary and praise the LORD.

    PSALM 134:2 NIV

WHAT THE BIBLE SAYS ABOUT WORSHIP

WORSHIP WITH DANCE

- Praise his name with dancing,
  accompanied by tambourine and harp.

  PSALM 149:3 NLT

- "Hear, O LORD, and be merciful to me;
  O LORD, be my help."
    You turned my wailing into dancing;
  you removed my sackcloth and clothed
  me with joy.

  PSALM 30:10–11 NIV

- Then Miriam the prophet, Aaron's sister, took
  a tambourine and led all the women as they
  played their tambourines and danced. And
  Miriam sang this song:
    "Sing to the LORD,
  for he has triumphed gloriously;
  he has hurled both horse and rider
  into the sea."

  EXODUS 15:20–21 NLT

WHAT THE BIBLE SAYS ABOUT WORSHIP

■ When those who were carrying the ark of the Lord had taken six steps, he sacrificed a bull and a fattened calf. David, wearing a linen ephod, danced before the Lord with all his might, while he and the entire house of Israel brought up the ark of the Lord with shouts and the sound of trumpets.

2 Samuel 6:13–15 niv

WHAT THE BIBLE SAYS ABOUT WORSHIP

WORSHIP WITH PRAYER

- The one thing I ask of the Lord—the thing I seek most—is to live in the house of the Lord all the days of my life, delighting in the Lord's perfections and meditating in his Temple.

    Psalm 27:4 NLT

- To God only wise, be glory through Jesus Christ for ever. Amen.

    Romans 16:27 KJV

- Grace to you and peace from God our Father and the Lord Jesus Christ, who gave Himself for our sins so that He might rescue us from this present evil age, according to the will of our God and Father, to whom be the glory forevermore. Amen.

    Galatians 1:3–5 NASB

WHAT THE BIBLE SAYS ABOUT WORSHIP

- Now unto him that is able to do exceeding abundantly above all that we ask or think, according to the power that worketh in us,
    Unto him be glory in the church by Christ Jesus throughout all ages, world without end. Amen.

    EPHESIANS 3:20–21 KJV

- May the God of peace, who through the blood of the eternal covenant brought back from the dead our Lord Jesus, that great Shepherd of the sheep, equip you with everything good for doing his will, and may he work in us what is pleasing to him, through Jesus Christ, to whom be glory for ever and ever. Amen.

    HEBREWS 13:20–21 NIV

- But grow in the grace and knowledge of our Lord and Savior Jesus Christ. To him be glory both now and forever! Amen.

    2 PETER 3:18 NIV

WHAT THE BIBLE SAYS ABOUT WORSHIP

- Saying, "Amen! Blessing and glory and wisdom and thanksgiving and honor and power and might be to our God forever and ever! Amen."

    REVELATION 7:12 ESV

- "The Lamb who was killed is worthy to receive power, riches, wisdom, strength, honor, glory, and praise. . . .

    "Praise, honor, glory, and strength forever and ever to the one who sits on the throne and to the Lamb!"

    REVELATION 5:12–13 CEV

WHAT THE BIBLE SAYS ABOUT WORSHIP

■ "Holy, holy, holy,
   Lord God Almighty,
   Who was and is and is to come!"

REVELATION 4:8 NKJV

ONE MOMENT AT A TIME

EXPANDING HORIZONS

- **Attend a new service.** When the opportunity presents itself, visit a church that has a different worship style than the one you're used to. The differences found in a liturgical, charismatic, or another unfamiliar style can expand your view of God and worship.

- **Try a prayer book.** Many liturgical prayer books can help you worship God using words or prayers that you haven't considered before. Add such a book to your devotional routine for a few weeks and allow it to broaden your perspective of praise.

- **Learn a new skill.** Teach yourself to play basic chords on the guitar (or pick up another instrument). Once you have some basics down, consider adding the instrument to your worship routine.

WHAT THE BIBLE SAYS ABOUT WORSHIP

CHAPTER 7
PERSONAL REASONS TO WORSHIP GOD

As a recent seminary graduate, I found that I approached worship very academically. I knew the history of church services, the benefits of worship, and our obligations in this area. What I had forgotten, and am learning to reclaim, is the personal nature of worship. God is worthy of worship because of what He's done for me. He loves me. He's forgiven me. With all the billions of people in the world to keep track of, He remembers and cares for me. God is certainly worthy of praise!

■ Toby, age 29, Washington, D.C. ■

WORSHIP BECAUSE OF HIS LOVE

- Because your love is better than life,
    my lips will glorify you.

    PSALM 63:3 NIV

- Give thanks to the LORD, for he is good;
    his love endures forever.

    1 CHRONICLES 16:34 NIV

- The LORD's lovingkindnesses indeed
    never cease,
  For His compassions never fail.
  They are new every morning;
  Great is Your faithfulness.

    LAMENTATIONS 3:22–23 NASB

WHAT THE BIBLE SAYS ABOUT WORSHIP

■ Your love, O Lord, reaches to the heavens,
  your faithfulness to the skies.
Your righteousness is like the mighty
  mountains, your justice like the
  great deep.
O Lord, you preserve both man and beast.

PSALM 36:5–6 NIV

■ For God is sheer beauty, all-generous in love,
loyal always and ever.

PSALM 100:5 MSG

■ How priceless is your unfailing love!
Both high and low among men find refuge
  in the shadow of your wings.

PSALM 36:7 NIV

■ The Lord appeared to us in the past, saying:
"I have loved you with an everlasting love;
I have drawn you with loving-kindness."

JEREMIAH 31:3 NIV

WHAT THE BIBLE SAYS ABOUT WORSHIP

- Know therefore that the LORD your God is God; he is the faithful God, keeping his covenant of love to a thousand generations of those who love him and keep his commands.

    DEUTERONOMY 7:9 NIV

WHAT THE BIBLE SAYS ABOUT WORSHIP

WORSHIP BECAUSE OF HIS ANSWERS TO PRAYER

- But God did listen!
  He paid attention to my prayer.
  Praise God, who did not ignore my prayer
  or withdraw his unfailing love from me.

  PSALM 66:19–20 NLT

- I call on you, O God, for you will answer me;
  give ear to me and hear my prayer.

  PSALM 17:6 NIV

- "I thank and praise you, O God of my fathers: You have given me wisdom and power, you have made known to me what we asked of you, you have made known to us the dream of the king."

  DANIEL 2:23 NIV

WHAT THE BIBLE SAYS ABOUT WORSHIP

■ The Lord has heard my plea;
the Lord will answer my prayer.

PSALM 6:9 NLT

■ I called on your name, O Lord,
   from the depths of the pit.
You heard my plea: "Do not close your ears
   to my cry for relief."
You came near when I called you,
   and you said, "Do not fear."
O Lord, you took up my case;
   you redeemed my life.

LAMENTATIONS 3:55–58 NIV

■ "Praise be to the Lord, who has given rest to his people Israel just as he promised. Not one word has failed of all the good promises he gave through his servant Moses."

1 KINGS 8:56 NIV

WHAT THE BIBLE SAYS ABOUT WORSHIP

- My soul makes its boast in the Lord;
    let the humble hear and be glad....
  I sought the Lord, and he answered me
    and delivered me from all my fears.

  PSALM 34:2, 4 ESV

- Then we cried out to the Lord, the God of our fathers, and the Lord heard our voice and saw our misery, toil and oppression.

  So the Lord brought us out of Egypt with a mighty hand and an outstretched arm, with great terror and with miraculous signs and wonders.

  DEUTERONOMY 26:7–8 NIV

WORSHIP BECAUSE OF HIS FORGIVENESS

■ He has paid a full ransom for his people. He has guaranteed his covenant with them forever. What a holy, awe-inspiring name he has!

    Psalm 111:9 nlt

■ Our Redeemer—the Lord Almighty is his name—is the Holy One of Israel.

    Isaiah 47:4 niv

■ "He redeemed my soul from going down to the pit, and I will live to enjoy the light."

    Job 33:28 niv

WHAT THE BIBLE SAYS ABOUT WORSHIP

- Who is a God like you, pardoning iniquity
    and passing over transgression for the
    remnant of his inheritance?
  He does not retain his anger forever,
    because he delights in steadfast love.
  He will again have compassion on us;
    he will tread our iniquities underfoot.
  You will cast all our sins into the depths of
    the sea.

  MICAH 7:18–19 ESV

- Give thanks to the LORD, for he is good!
  His faithful love endures forever.
  Has the LORD redeemed you? Then speak out!
  Tell others he has redeemed you from your
  enemies.

  PSALM 107:1–2 NLT

- Praise the LORD…who forgives all your sins
  and heals all your diseases.

  PSALM 103:1, 3 NIV

WHAT THE BIBLE SAYS ABOUT WORSHIP

> He will not constantly accuse us,
>   nor remain angry forever.
> He does not punish us for all our sins;
>   he does not deal harshly with us,
>   as we deserve.
> For his unfailing love toward those who
>   fear him is as great as the height of
>   the heavens above the earth.
> He has removed our sins as far from us
>   as the east is from the west.
> The Lord is like a father to his children,
>   tender and compassionate to those
>   who fear him.
>
> Psalm 103:9–13 nlt

WHAT THE BIBLE SAYS ABOUT WORSHIP

■ Who may ascend the hill of the Lord?
Who may stand in his holy place?
He who has clean hands and a pure heart,
   who does not lift up his soul to an idol
   or swear by what is false.
He will receive blessing from the Lord
   and vindication from God his Savior.

PSALM 24:3–5 NIV

WHAT THE BIBLE SAYS ABOUT WORSHIP

WORSHIP BECAUSE OF HIS MERCY AND GRACE

- Praise be to the God and Father of our Lord Jesus Christ! In his great mercy he has given us new birth into a living hope through the resurrection of Jesus Christ from the dead.

    1 Peter 1:3 niv

- "If you return to the Lord, then your brothers and your children will be shown compassion by their captors and will come back to this land, for the Lord your God is gracious and compassionate. He will not turn his face from you if you return to him."

    2 Chronicles 30:9 niv

WHAT THE BIBLE SAYS ABOUT WORSHIP

- Therefore the Lord waits to be gracious to you, and therefore he exalts himself to show mercy to you. For the Lord is a God of justice; blessed are all those who wait for him.

  Isaiah 30:18 esv

- But you, O Lord, are a God merciful and gracious, slow to anger and abounding in steadfast love and faithfulness.

  Psalm 86:15 esv

- Have mercy on me, O God,
      because of your unfailing love.
  Because of your great compassion,
      blot out the stain of my sins.

  Psalm 51:1 nlt

WHAT THE BIBLE SAYS ABOUT WORSHIP

■ I love the Lord, because he has heard my voice and my pleas for mercy.

PSALM 116:1 ESV

■ God is sheer mercy and grace; not easily angered, he's rich in love.

PSALM 103:8 MSG

WHAT THE BIBLE SAYS ABOUT WORSHIP

WORSHIP BECAUSE OF HIS SALVATION

- Sing to the LORD, all the earth;
    proclaim his salvation day after day.

    1 CHRONICLES 16:23 NIV

- I will praise You,
    For You have answered me,
    And have become my salvation.

    PSALM 118:21 NKJV

- "The LORD is my strength and my song;
    he has become my salvation.
  He is my God, and I will praise him,
    my father's God, and I will exalt him."

    EXODUS 15:2 NIV

WHAT THE BIBLE SAYS ABOUT WORSHIP

- Praise be to the God and Father of our Lord Jesus Christ, who has blessed us in the heavenly realms with every spiritual blessing in Christ. For he chose us in him before the creation of the world to be holy and blameless in his sight. In love he predestined us to be adopted as his sons through Jesus Christ, in accordance with his pleasure and will—to the praise of his glorious grace, which he has freely given us in the One he loves. In him we have redemption through his blood, the forgiveness of sins, in accordance with the riches of God's grace.

    EPHESIANS 1:3–7 NIV

- The ransomed of the LORD will return.
  They will enter Zion with singing;
      everlasting joy will crown their heads.
  Gladness and joy will overtake them,
      and sorrow and sighing will flee away.

    ISAIAH 51:11 NIV

WHAT THE BIBLE SAYS ABOUT WORSHIP

■ Our Lord, let your worshipers
    rejoice and be glad.
They love you for saving them,
    so let them always say,
"The Lord is wonderful!"

PSALM 40:16 CEV

■ My soul finds rest in God alone;
    my salvation comes from him.
He alone is my rock and my salvation;
    he is my fortress, I will never be shaken.

PSALM 62:1–2 NIV

■ And it will be said in that day,
    "Behold, this is our God for whom we
    have waited that He might save us.
This is the Lord for whom we have waited;
    Let us rejoice and be glad in His
    salvation."

ISAIAH 25:9 NASB

WHAT THE BIBLE SAYS ABOUT WORSHIP

■ I pray that you will be grateful to God for letting you have part in what he has promised his people in the kingdom of light.

> COLOSSIANS 1:12 CEV

■ But thanks be to God, who always leads us in triumphal procession in Christ and through us spreads everywhere the fragrance of the knowledge of him.

> 2 CORINTHIANS 2:14 NIV

WHAT THE BIBLE SAYS ABOUT WORSHIP

WORSHIP BECAUSE OF HIS HELP

- Praise be to the Lord, to God our Savior, who daily bears our burdens.

  PSALM 68:19 NIV

- Sing to the LORD! Give praise to the LORD! He rescues the life of the needy from the hands of the wicked.

  JEREMIAH 20:13 NIV

- Praise the LORD, all you who fear him!
  Honor him, all you descendants of Jacob!
  Show him reverence, all you descendants
     of Israel!
  For he has not ignored or belittled the
     suffering of the needy.
  He has not turned his back on them,
     but has listened to their cries for help.

  PSALM 22:23–24 NLT

WHAT THE BIBLE SAYS ABOUT WORSHIP

■ I will give thanks to the LORD with all my
   heart; I will tell of all Your wonders....
When my enemies turn back,
   They stumble and perish before You.

PSALM 9:1, 3 NASB

■ The LORD lives, and blessed be my rock;
And exalted be the God of my salvation,
The God who executes vengeance for me,
And subdues peoples under me.
   He delivers me from my enemies;
Surely You lift me above those who rise
up against me; You rescue me from the
violent man.

PSALM 18:46–48 NASB

WHAT THE BIBLE SAYS ABOUT WORSHIP

■ Blessed be the Lord! For he has heard the voice of my pleas for mercy.

    The Lord is my strength and my shield; in him my heart trusts, and I am helped; my heart exults, and with my song I give thanks to him.

Psalm 28:6–7 ESV

WHAT THE BIBLE SAYS ABOUT WORSHIP

WORSHIP BECAUSE OF HIS COMFORT

- How kind the Lord is! How good he is! So merciful, this God of ours!

  PSALM 116:5 NLT

- God blesses those people who grieve. They will find comfort!

  MATTHEW 5:4 CEV

- All praise to God, the Father of our Lord Jesus Christ. God is our merciful Father and the source of all comfort. He comforts us in all our troubles so that we can comfort others. When they are troubled, we will be able to give them the same comfort God has given us. For the more we suffer for Christ, the more God will shower us with his comfort through Christ.

  2 CORINTHIANS 1:3–5 NLT

WHAT THE BIBLE SAYS ABOUT WORSHIP

- In that day you will sing:
  "I will praise you, O Lord!
  You were angry with me, but not any more.
  Now you comfort me."

  Isaiah 12:1 NLT

- God our Father loves us. He is kind and has given us eternal comfort and a wonderful hope.

  2 Thessalonians 2:16 CEV

- The Lord is good to all; he has compassion
    on all he has made.
  All you have made will praise you, O Lord;
    your saints will extol you.

  Psalm 145:9–10 NIV

- Let the ruins of Jerusalem break into joyful song, for the Lord has comforted his people. He has redeemed Jerusalem.

  Isaiah 52:9 NLT

WHAT THE BIBLE SAYS ABOUT WORSHIP

- The LORD cares for his nation, just as shepherds care for their flocks. He carries the lambs in his arms, while gently leading the mother sheep.

    ISAIAH 40:11 CEV

WORSHIP BECAUSE OF HIS PROVISION

- When you have eaten and are satisfied, praise the LORD your God for the good land he has given you.

    DEUTERONOMY 8:10 NIV

- "Then this city will bring me renown, joy, praise and honor before all nations on earth that hear of all the good things I do for it; and they will be in awe and will tremble at the abundant prosperity and peace I provide for it."

    JEREMIAH 33:9 NIV

- You care for the land and water it; you enrich it abundantly. The streams of God are filled with water to provide the people with grain, for so you have ordained it.

    PSALM 65:9 NIV

WHAT THE BIBLE SAYS ABOUT WORSHIP

■ Great are the works of the LORD; they are pondered by all who delight in them....

  He provides food for those who fear him; he remembers his covenant forever.

PSALM 111:2, 5 NIV

■ But remember the LORD your God, for it is he who gives you the ability to produce wealth, and so confirms his covenant, which he swore to your forefathers, as it is today.

DEUTERONOMY 8:18 NIV

■ Every good and perfect gift is from above, coming down from the Father of the heavenly lights, who does not change like shifting shadows.

JAMES 1:17 NIV

WHAT THE BIBLE SAYS ABOUT WORSHIP

- By his divine power, God has given us everything we need for living a godly life. We have received all of this by coming to know him, the one who called us to himself by means of his marvelous glory and excellence.

    2 PETER 1:3 NLT

- GOD will lavish you with good things: children from your womb, offspring from your animals, and crops from your land, the land that GOD promised your ancestors that he would give you. GOD will throw open the doors of his sky vaults and pour rain on your land on schedule and bless the work you take in hand. You will lend to many nations but you yourself won't have to take out a loan.

    DEUTERONOMY 28:11–12 MSG

WHAT THE BIBLE SAYS ABOUT WORSHIP

WORSHIP BECAUSE OF HIS GOOD WORKS

- You did it: You changed wild lament into whirling dance; you ripped off my black mourning band and decked me with wildflowers.

  I'm about to burst with song; I can't keep quiet about you. GOD, my God, I can't thank you enough.

  PSALM 30:11–12 MSG

- From the end of the earth I call to you
    when my heart is faint.
  Lead me to the rock that is higher than I,
  for you have been my refuge, a strong tower
  against the enemy. . . .

  For you, O God, have heard my vows;
  you have given me the heritage of those who
  fear your name.

  PSALM 61:2–3, 5 ESV

WHAT THE BIBLE SAYS ABOUT WORSHIP

- O Lord, You are my God; I will exalt You,
  I will give thanks to Your name; for You have
  worked wonders, plans formed long ago,
  with perfect faithfulness.

  Isaiah 25:1 nasb

- Praise the Lord God, the God of Israel,
  who alone does such wonderful things.

  Psalm 72:18 nlt

- Sing to him, sing praise to him;
  tell of all his wonderful acts.

  Psalm 105:2 niv

- Sing praises to the Lord, enthroned in Zion;
  proclaim among the nations what he has
  done.

  Psalm 9:11 niv

- You made me so happy, God.
  I saw your work and I shouted for joy.

  Psalm 92:4 msg

WHAT THE BIBLE SAYS ABOUT WORSHIP

- I wash my hands in innocence, and go about your altar, O Lord, proclaiming aloud your praise and telling of all your wonderful deeds.

    PSALM 26:6–7 NIV

- I will praise you forever for what you have done; in your name I will hope, for your name is good. I will praise you in the presence of your saints.

    PSALM 52:9 NIV

- Bless the Lord, O my soul. . .who crowns you with steadfast love and mercy, who satisfies you with good so that your youth is renewed like the eagle's.

    PSALM 103:2, 4–5 ESV

WHAT THE BIBLE SAYS ABOUT WORSHIP

- May the peoples praise you, O God;
  may all the peoples praise you.
  May the nations be glad and sing for joy,
  for you rule the peoples justly
  and guide the nations of the earth.

  PSALM 67:3–4 NIV

- One generation will commend your works to another; they will tell of your mighty acts.

  They will speak of the glorious splendor of your majesty, and I will meditate on your wonderful works.

  They will tell of the power of your awesome works, and I will proclaim your great deeds.

  They will celebrate your abundant goodness and joyfully sing of your righteousness.

  PSALM 145:4–7 NIV

WHAT THE BIBLE SAYS ABOUT WORSHIP

WORSHIP BECAUSE OF HIS WORD

- Seven times a day I praise you
  for your righteous laws.

  PSALM 119:164 NIV

- I praise God for what he has promised.
  I trust in God, so why should I be afraid?
  What can mere mortals do to me? ...
     I praise God for what he has promised;
  Yes, I praise the LORD for what he has
  promised.

  PSALM 56:4, 10 NLT

- I will praise you with an upright heart
     as I learn your righteous laws.
  I will obey your decrees; do not utterly
     forsake me.

  PSALM 119:7–8 NIV

WHAT THE BIBLE SAYS ABOUT WORSHIP

- All Scripture is inspired by God and is useful to teach us what is true and to make us realize what is wrong in our lives. It corrects us when we are wrong and teaches us to do what is right. God uses it to prepare and equip his people to do every good work.

   2 Timothy 3:16–17 NLT

- I have hidden your word in my heart
    that I might not sin against you.
  Praise be to you, O Lord;
    teach me your decrees.

   Psalm 119:11–12 NIV

- Accept, O Lord, the willing praise of my
    mouth, and teach me your laws.
  Though I constantly take my life in my hands,
    I will not forget your law.

   Psalm 119:108–109 NIV

WHAT THE BIBLE SAYS ABOUT WORSHIP

■ What God has said isn't only alive and active! It is sharper than any double-edged sword. His word can cut through our spirits and souls and through our joints and marrow, until it discovers the desires and thoughts of our hearts.

HEBREWS 4:12 CEV

WHAT THE BIBLE SAYS ABOUT WORSHIP

WORSHIP BECAUSE OF HIS PROTECTION AND STRENGTH

- You who fear the Lord, trust in the Lord;
  He is their help and their shield.

  PSALM 115:11 NASB

- O my Strength, I sing praise to you;
  you, O God, are my fortress, my loving God.

  PSALM 59:17 NIV

- May he be enthroned in God's presence forever; appoint your love and faithfulness to protect him.

  Then will I ever sing praise to your name and fulfill my vows day after day.

  PSALM 61:7–8 NIV

WHAT THE BIBLE SAYS ABOUT WORSHIP

■ I am in pain and distress; may your salvation,
O God, protect me.

   I will praise God's name in song and
glorify him with thanksgiving.

Psalm 69:29–30 niv

■ Whom have I in heaven but you?
And earth has nothing I desire besides you.

   My flesh and my heart may fail,
but God is the strength of my heart
and my portion forever.

   Those who are far from you will perish;
you destroy all who are unfaithful to you.

   But as for me, it is good to be near God.
I have made the Sovereign Lord my refuge;
I will tell of all your deeds.

Psalm 73:25–28 niv

WHAT THE BIBLE SAYS ABOUT WORSHIP

- "The Lord is my rock, my fortress, and my savior; my God is my rock, in whom I find protection.

    He is my shield, the power that saves me, and my place of safety.

    He is my refuge, my savior, the one who saves me from violence.

    I called on the Lord, who is worthy of praise, and he saved me from my enemies."

    2 Samuel 22:2–4 nlt

- The Lord reigns forever; he has established his throne for judgment.

    He will judge the world in righteousness; he will govern the peoples with justice.

    The Lord is a refuge for the oppressed, a stronghold in times of trouble.

    Those who know your name will trust in you, for you, Lord, have never forsaken those who seek you.

    Psalm 9:7–10 niv

WHAT THE BIBLE SAYS ABOUT WORSHIP

- You are awesome, O God, in your sanctuary; the God of Israel gives power and strength to his people. Praise be to God!

    PSALM 68:35 NIV

- I praise you, LORD, for answering my prayers. You are my strong shield, and I trust you completely.

    You have helped me, and I will celebrate and thank you in song.

    PSALM 28:6–7 CEV

- O LORD my God, in You I have taken refuge;
    Save me from all those who pursue me,
    and deliver me.

    PSALM 7:1 NASB

- I have been young, and now am old,
    yet I have not seen the righteous forsaken
    or his children begging for bread.

    PSALM 37:25 ESV

WHAT THE BIBLE SAYS ABOUT WORSHIP

■ Five sparrows are sold for just two pennies, but God doesn't forget a one of them. Even the hairs on your head are counted. So don't be afraid! You are worth much more than many sparrows.

Luke 12:6–7 CEV

ONE MOMENT AT A TIME

PERSONAL REFLECTIONS

- **Create a cross.** Get a pad of sticky notes and write one personal reason to praise God on each one. Arrange the notes in the shape of a cross and thank God for the reasons He's given you to praise Him.

- **Encourage your family.** If you don't do so already, take regular time as a family to praise God together. Share prayer requests, answers, and lessons He's teaching you that encourage you to praise.

- **Create a mix.** Create a CD or playlist on your MP3 player that reminds you of attributes of God and His work in your life. Use these reminders to drive you to worship Him.

WHAT THE BIBLE SAYS ABOUT WORSHIP

CHAPTER 8
EXAMPLES OF WORSHIP

Since I had never thought much about it, I used to think that worship was limited to what I did at church. I'd sit reverently, sing on cue, and listen attentively—at least, I'd try to. But I'm learning that worship is much more than what happens on Sunday mornings. The Bible talks about people who worshipped God outside of church in some unusual ways. Some danced before God, others wept in front of others, and still others sang hymns while chained to a jail floor. The more I learn, the more I realize my views of worship have been too limited.

■ Mika, age 23, Illinois ■

WHAT THE BIBLE SAYS ABOUT WORSHIP

WORSHIP WITHOUT NEEDING SOCIAL APPROVAL

■ The Ark of the Lord remained there in Obed-edom's house for three months, and the Lord blessed Obed-edom and his entire household.

Then King David was told, "The Lord has blessed Obed-edom's household and everything he has because of the Ark of God." So David went there and brought the Ark...to the City of David with a great celebration. After the men who were carrying [it] had gone six steps, David sacrificed a bull and a fattened calf. And David danced before the Lord with all his might, wearing a priestly garment. So David and all...Israel brought up the Ark of the Lord with shouts of joy and the blowing of rams' horns.

2 Samuel 6:11–15 nlt

WHAT THE BIBLE SAYS ABOUT WORSHIP

■ Now one of the Pharisees was requesting [Jesus] to dine with him, and He entered the Pharisee's house and reclined at the table. And there was a woman in the city who was a sinner; and when she learned that He was reclining at the table in the Pharisee's house, she brought an alabaster vial of perfume, and standing behind Him at His feet, weeping, she began to wet His feet with her tears, and kept wiping them with the hair of her head, and kissing His feet and anointing them with the perfume.... Then He said to her, "Your sins have been forgiven.... Your faith has saved you; go in peace."

LUKE 7:36–38, 48, 50 NASB

WHAT THE BIBLE SAYS ABOUT WORSHIP

WORSHIP DURING DIFFICULT TIMES

■ They seized Paul and Silas and...commanded them to be beaten with rods. And when they had laid many stripes on them, they threw them into prison, commanding the jailer to keep them securely. Having received such a charge, he put them into the inner prison and fastened their feet in the stocks.

But at midnight Paul and Silas were praying and singing hymns to God, and the prisoners were listening to them. Suddenly there was a great earthquake, so that the foundations of the prison were shaken; and immediately all the doors were opened and everyone's chains were loosed. And the keeper of the prison, awaking from sleep and seeing the prison doors open, supposing the prisoners had fled, drew his sword and was about to kill himself. But Paul called with a loud voice, saying, "Do yourself no harm,

WHAT THE BIBLE SAYS ABOUT WORSHIP

for we are all here." Then he called for a light, ran in, and fell down trembling before Paul and Silas. And he brought them out and said, "Sirs, what must I do to be saved?" So they said, "Believe on the Lord Jesus Christ, and you will be saved, you and your household."

ACTS 16:19, 22–31 NKJV

WHAT THE BIBLE SAYS ABOUT WORSHIP

WORSHIP THROUGH GRIEF

- There was a man in the land of Uz whose name was Job, and that man was blameless and upright, one who feared God and turned away from evil. There were born to him seven sons and three daughters. He possessed 7,000 sheep, 3,000 camels, 500 yoke of oxen, and 500 female donkeys, and very many servants, so that this man was the greatest of all the people of the east....

  Now there was a day when...there came a messenger to Job and said, "The oxen were plowing and the donkeys feeding beside them, and the Sabeans fell upon them and took them and struck down the servants with the edge of the sword, and I alone have escaped to tell you." While he was yet speaking, there came another and said, "The fire of God fell from heaven and burned up the sheep and the servants and consumed them, and I alone have escaped to tell you." While

WHAT THE BIBLE SAYS ABOUT WORSHIP

he was yet speaking, there came another and said, "The Chaldeans formed three groups and made a raid on the camels and took them and struck down the servants with the edge of the sword, and I alone have escaped to tell you." While he was yet speaking, there came another and said, "Your sons and daughters were eating and drinking wine in their oldest brother's house, and behold, a great wind came across the wilderness and struck the four corners of the house, and it fell upon the young people, and they are dead, and I alone have escaped to tell you."

Then Job arose and tore his robe and shaved his head and fell on the ground and worshiped. And he said, "Naked I came from my mother's womb, and naked shall I return. The LORD gave, and the LORD has taken away; blessed be the name of the LORD."

JOB 1:1–3, 21 ESV

WHAT THE BIBLE SAYS ABOUT WORSHIP

WORSHIP ON THE BATTLEFIELD

- When Gideon [was spying on his enemy's camp], behold, a man was telling a dream to his comrade. And he said, "Behold, I dreamed a dream, and behold, a cake of barley bread tumbled into the camp of Midian and came to the tent and struck it so that it fell and turned it upside down, so that the tent lay flat." And his comrade answered, "This is no other than the sword of Gideon the son of Joash, a man of Israel; God has given into his hand Midian and all the camp."

    As soon as Gideon heard the telling of the dream and its interpretation, he worshiped. And he returned to the camp of Israel and said, "Arise, for the LORD has given the host of Midian into your hand."

    JUDGES 7:13–15 ESV

WHAT THE BIBLE SAYS ABOUT WORSHIP

WORSHIP BEFORE A GREAT UNDERTAKING

■ When the builders laid the foundation of the temple of the LORD, the priests in their vestments and with trumpets, and the Levites (the sons of Asaph) with cymbals, took their places to praise the LORD, as prescribed by David king of Israel. With praise and thanksgiving they sang to the LORD:

"He is good; his love to Israel endures forever." And all the people gave a great shout of praise to the LORD, because the foundation of the house of the LORD was laid.

EZRA 3:10–11 NIV

ONE MOMENT AT A TIME

EXPRESSING YOURSELF

- **Look beyond the hymnbook.** Worship at church and through songs is very valuable. But what unexpected—even routine—events do you have coming up that can provide a place for you to worship God?

- **Concern yourself with God.** Our concern for what others will think can affect what we wear to church or how we act while we're there. Worship passionately and without fear of what others might think.

- **Bring worship with you in difficult times.** Stress, grief, and pain may not seem like traditional times to worship, but focusing on God during these times can be life changing. Follow examples from Jonah, David, and Job who worshipped during their most troubling circumstances.

Look for all the
What the Bible Says about…
books from Barbour Publishing

What the Bible Says about
GOD'S WILL
ISBN 978-1-60260-279-3

What the Bible Says about
EMOTIONS
ISBN 978-1-60260-281-6

What the Bible Says about
PRAYING
ISBN 978-1-60260-282-3

192 pages / 3 ¾" x 6" / $4.97 each

Available wherever Christian books are sold.